BASKETBALL LEGENDS

Kareem Abdul-Jabbar
Charles Barkley
Larry Bird
Kobe Bryant
Wilt Chamberlain
Clyde Drexler
Julius Erving
Patrick Ewing
Kevin Garnett
Anfernee Hardaway
Tim Hardaway
The Head Coaches
Grant Hill
Juwan Howard
Allen Iverson
Magic Johnson
Michael Jordan
Shawn Kemp
Jason Kidd
Reggie Miller
Alonzo Mourning
Hakeem Olajuwon
Shaquille O'Neal
Gary Payton
Scottie Pippen
David Robinson
Dennis Rodman
John Stockton
Keith Van Horn
Antoine Walker
Chris Webber

CHELSEA HOUSE PUBLISHERS

BASKETBALL LEGENDS

ALLEN IVERSON

Charles E. Schmidt Jr.

Introduction by
Chuck Daly

CHELSEA HOUSE PUBLISHERS
Philadelphia

Produced by Duke & Company
Devon, Pennsylvania

General Editor: Gerald Zeigerman
Senior Consulting Editor: Benjamin Cohen
Junior Consulting Editor: Jake Schlessinger
Picture Research: Sandy Jones
Cover Illustration: Earl Parker

3 5 7 9 8 6 4 2

The Chelsea House World Wide Web address is
http://www.chelseahouse.com

Library of Congress Cataloging-in-Publication Data

Schmidt, Charles E., Jr.
  Allen Iverson / by Charles E. Schmidt, Jr.
    p. cm.
  Includes bibliographical references (p.) and index.
  Summary: Traces the personal life and basketball career of the high-scoring
rookie with the Philadelphia 76ers, Allen Iverson.
  ISBN 0-7910-4852-7
  1. Iverson, Allen, 1975-   —Juvenile literature. 2. Basketball players—United
States—Biography—Juvenile literature. 3. Philadelphia 76ers (Basketball
team)—Juvenile literature. [1. Iverson, Allen, 1975-   . 2. Basketball players.
3. Afro-Americans—
  Biography.] I. Title.
  GV884.I84S35   1997
  796.323'092—dc21   97-33159
  [B]   CIP
                                                       AC

CONTENTS

Becoming a Basketball Legend

Chuck Daly

What does it take to be a basketball superstar? Two of the three things it takes are easy to spot. Any great athlete must have excellent skills and tremendous dedication. The third quality needed is much harder to define, or even put in words. Others call it leadership or desire to win, but I'm not sure that explains it fully. This third quality relates to the athlete's thinking process, a certain mentality and work ethic. One can coach athletic skills, and while few superstars need outside influence to help keep them dedicated, it is possible for a coach to offer some well-timed words in order to keep that athlete fully motivated. But a coach can do no more than appeal to a player's will to win; how much that player is then capable of ensuring victory is up to his own internal workings.

In recent times, we have been fortunate to have seen some of the best to play the game. Larry Bird, Magic Johnson, and Michael Jordan had all three components of superstardom in full measure. They brought their teams to numerous championships, and made the players around them better. (They also made their coaches look smart.)

I myself coached a player who belongs in that class, Isiah Thomas, who helped lead the Detroit Pistons to two consecutive NBA crowns. Isiah is not tall—he's just over six feet—but he could do whatever he wanted with the ball. And what he wanted to do most was lead and win.

All the players I mentioned above and those whom this series will chronicle are tremendously gifted athletes, but for the most part, you can't play professional basketball at all unless you have excellent skills. And few players get to stay on their team unless they are willing to dedicate themselves to improving their talents even more, learning about their opponents, and finding a way to join with their teammates and win.

It's that third element that separates the good player from the superstar, the memorable players from the legends of the game. Superstars know when to take over the game. If the situation calls for a defensive stop, the superstars stand up and do it. If the situation calls for a big shot, they want the ball. They don't want the ball simply because of their own glory or ego. Instead they know—and their teammates know—that they are the ones who can deliver, regardless of the pressure.

The words "legend" and "superstar" are often tossed around without real meaning. Taking a hard look at some of those who truly can be classified as "legends" can provide insight into the things that brought them to that level. All of them developed their legacy over numerous seasons of play, even if certain games will always stand out in the memories of those who saw them. Those games typically featured amazing feats of all-around play. No matter how great the fans thought the superstars, the players were capable yet of surprising them, their opponents, and occasionally even themselves. The desire to win took over, and with their dedication and athletic skills already in place, they were capable of the most astonishing achievements.

CHUCK DALY, most recently the head coach of the New Jersey Nets, guided the Detroit Pistons to two straight NBA championships, in 1989 and 1990. He earned a gold medal as coach of the 1992 U.S. Olympic basketball team—the so-called "Dream Team"—and was inducted into the Pro Basketball Hall of Fame in 1994.

SEARCHING FOR "THE ANSWER"

With the unmistakable *swish* of a basketball hitting nothing but net, Allen Iverson of the Philadelphia 76ers completed the first leg of a sometimes rocky journey. This journey brought him from the playgrounds of Hampton, Virginia, to the heights of National Basketball Association (NBA) celebrity. Iverson is worthy of breathing the same rarefied air as the new generation of such stars as Damon Stoudamire, Kerry Kittles, Kobe Bryant, Marcus Camby, and Grant Hill. His on-court brilliance has led some observers to go so far as to say he will assume the mantle of His Airness, Michael Jordan, as the premier player of his generation.

That basket came with only seconds left in the April 14, 1997, game against the Washington Bullets. It gave Allen Iverson his 39th and 40th points and made it the fifth straight game in

Iverson passes the ball off as he is guarded by the Orlando Magic's Derek Strong, in Orlando, Florida, April 1, 1997. Iverson set a new record for most points scored by a rookie 76er in one year.

which he broke the 40-point barrier. This is a feat rarely accomplished by most players and never before by a rookie. The Washington game was preceded by a career-high 50-point outing against the Cleveland Cavaliers, 44 points against the Milwaukee Bucks, 40 points against the Atlanta Hawks, and 44 points against none other than the world champion Chicago Bulls. Each performance featured Iverson's dynamic, full-speed playing style that made him the smallest first-overall draft pick in the history of the NBA.

For such a record-setting performance, Iverson, whose nickname, "The Answer," is tattooed on his left arm, was named NBA Rookie of the Month for April. He also earned this honor for November, his first month in the league. His eventual selection as Schick Rookie of the Year for the 1996–97 season was a foregone conclusion.

But at 22, is Iverson heir apparent to Jordan or just another pretender to the throne? Both his personal life and his fledgling professional career have been marked by acts of kindness and heroic individual athletic feats, but they have also been marred by outbursts all too characteristic of the new generation of basketball player. Iverson's "jack-it-up-first" style of play has been described as selfish. His on-court brashness has tempered the praise for his scoring brilliance with criticism—often from unexpected sources. Rebukes have come not only from the press but from his peers and elder statesmen in the league as well.

Jordan himself has gone so far as to use Iverson as an example when discussing his dismay with the new generation of ballplayers. He feels they lack what he calls "respect for the game" and its established players.

For Iverson, however, his style of play is as much a part of him as eating and breathing.

"I wish I wasn't the one singled out," Iverson says. "The older guys get this idea about me from what they read in the papers. None of them have ever sat down and talked to me, and I think that's unfair. I have more love for this game than almost anyone, and that's the only thing that hurts, that they think I don't have respect for the game."

2

TOUGH
BEGINNINGS

To get to know Allen Iverson, you have to go back to his childhood years. That was when he developed the skills and mind-set that make him what he is today.

Allen grew up in a single-parent household in a poverty-stricken section of Hampton, Virginia. Located in the southeast corner of the state, Hampton sits at the mouth of the Chesapeake Bay near the vast naval shipyards of Newport News. When he was born, on June 7, 1975, his mother, Ann, was 16 and living with her grandmother. Allen's biological father vanished soon after his birth. Unskilled and alone, Ann tried her best to raise her young son, even though she was forced to move from one low-income neighborhood to another throughout his young life. Times were hard for both of them. Some of Allen's earliest memories are of his mother struggling to make an overdue utility bill payment before the water or electricity was shut off.

Iverson scores a touchdown for Bethel High School, Hampton, Virginia, on November 6, 1992.

Growing up in Hampton was dangerous. Allen saw violence—shootings, gang fights, drug use —all the time. When he was 14, his best friend was stabbed to death. Once, at a party in a hotel, someone was shot and killed. To make matters worse, the man he calls "Dad," who was not his biological father but the person who helped raise him, was arrested for selling cocaine. He ended up serving two prison terms. Allen explains that the man lost his shipyard job and only sold the drugs to try to get money for the family.

"I feel all the jail time he did was for us. He couldn't stand to see us living like that, so he went out and did what he had to do."

When Allen visited Dad in prison, he noticed the poor condition of his shoes. Allen bent down, took off his own shoes, and gave them to him. He went home barefoot.

Because his home life was so hard, Allen turned to the playing fields and courts for relief. And that's where he started to get a sense of who he was. Throughout his life, sports have been a constant for him—a source of safety and stability in his often tumultuous life. Sports also come easily to him. He excelled as a pitcher in baseball, a quarterback in football, and a guard in basketball. And he was always at the center of the action, always controlling the flow of the game, always looking to get the ball in a tight situation.

Despite the fame and fortune his natural ability to play basketball has brought him, when he was younger Allen saw himself more as a football star. Basketball was just a hobby, something to do when the weather got too cold to play football, his first love. He was never happier than when he was darting through a hole in the defensive line, faking a defensive back out of his shoes, and racing down a sideline to the roar of the crowd.

"I always figured I was going to go to one of those big football schools. Florida State. Notre Dame. Football was my first love. Still is. I was going to go to one of those schools and play both [football and basketball]. I just loved running the option, faking, throwing the ball, everything about football. I didn't even want to play basketball at first. I thought it was soft. My mother's the one who made me go to tryouts [when he was eight]. I'll thank her forever. I came back and said: 'I like basketball, too.'"

Ann herself was a varsity player on the Bethel High School girls' basketball team in the 1970s, in Hampton. She knew firsthand the thrill of the game. So she took it upon herself to teach her son its finer points. In the back of her mind, she feared the toll that the heavy physical contact of football might take on him. Some mothers and sons bond through bedtime stories and dinner-table conversations, but Ann and Allen shared a soft shooting touch and a mean crossover dribble. Many a morning, mother and son were the first to claim a playground court, while late-evening shoot-arounds often carried on well past dark.

Ann had a plan for her oldest child. It didn't include stuffy, one-room apartments with faulty plumbing and drug dealers in the hallway. An athlete herself, she realized that despite her son's love of football, his small size made it a long shot that he would find fame and fortune, much less earn a living, on the gridiron. But basketball— that was a sport where a talented individual, especially one who was fast and court-wise, could find a niche. So she turned to what she knew

best—shooting a ball into a hoop—and set out to teach Allen everything she could about the game. As a young, single mother, she herself had not experienced enough of life yet to pass on its lessons to her son. Still, she could pass on the tricks and wisdom she learned in the countless games she played on the court and in the playground.

"His cousins and uncles taught him to dribble the ball, but his mom taught him ball handling and the whole feel of the game," says Dwayne Campbell, one of Allen's childhood friends. "She was the one who taught him to go inside and drive for the hole."

Another person who was eager to help mold the athletically gifted boy into a determined young man was Gary Moore, his elementary-school football coach. Moore ran his programs with discipline. He emphasized academics and responsibility as components of winning. Allen flourished under his guidance. When Allen was 16, his mother moved out of the Bethel High School district. It meant he would no longer be eligible to play sports there. But Gary Moore came through for him. Because the two had become so close, Moore invited Allen to move into his home, where he stayed for almost a year.

Allen Iverson's mother had a dream that someday her son would play basketball. Seeing him in his Georgetown Hoyas' uniform was the beginning of her dream come true.

3

DOWN A
BLIND ALLEY

The cold, hard steel of the basketball rim vibrating in his hands. The crowd roaring in shocked appreciation. The vanquished look in the eyes of the opponent guarding him. All of these sensations are indelibly etched in Iverson's mind's eye. "This is *it*," he said to himself.

It was very impressive. His first dunk of a basketball in an organized game. At the tender age of 15, no less. Not bad for a skinny point guard from the projects who couldn't afford the new, fancy, name-brand sneakers the other kids had.

But Allen was a fast learner. He took what his mother taught him and started putting it to good use immediately. In organized games in elementary school and summer leagues, he was easily the most experienced player on the floor. He dominated opponents with his quickness and superior ball-handling ability. In informal pickup

In 1994, Iverson was asked if he could ever put it all behind him—the jail time, the jeering fans, the legal wrangling that finally cleared his name. "I'm over it," he replied, without missing a beat.

games at the playground, he was always among the first to be picked. More than once, a minor scuffle broke out between team captains. Each one wanted first pick in order to choose Iverson.

Because of his scoring ability and court sense, people said that he "played taller" than he really was. Add to this mix his explosive quickness and, even before he reached high school, Allen was a minor celebrity on the playgrounds of Hampton. Everyone knew "Bubbachuck," his childhood nickname. If you had him on your team, you were almost guaranteed a win, no matter what the sport.

Although he was a prolific scorer, coaches were quick to recognize the ability and poise that helped Iverson keep his cool under the pressure of a tight game situation. This characteristic prompted them to place him at point guard, a position not known for producing high scoring numbers. Traditionally, the point guard is a basketball team's "quarterback," the player who brings the ball up court, positions his teammates, and calls the planned play, usually passing the ball to a forward or center, who then takes a shot.

Allen gravitated naturally to the position. It suited his need to be at the center of the action and in control of a situation. It didn't take long for him to modify the position to fit his style of play. Because it was successful, no one minded.

In his junior year of high school, Allen led the Bethel High School basketball team to a state championship by averaging 31.6 points per game. He also led the football squad to a state crown. He passed for 1,423 yards, rushed for 781 yards, and scored 34 touchdowns. For these accomplishments, he was named Virginia High School Player of the Year in both sports by the Associated Press.

When Allen led his summer-league Amateur

Athletic Union (AAU) team to a national championship, he was voted the tournament's most valuable player. His competition? Joe Smith, who went on to be a standout at the University of Maryland, and Jerry Stackhouse, Allen's teammate and fellow number-one draft pick on the 76ers.

"I've known him 14, 15 years," says Dwayne Campbell. "I knew he was a good athlete in Aberdeen Elementary School, when we started getting our first football teams together. Right then, I saw this bony little kid out there doing all the things the big kids could. Right then, I knew something was going to happen."

Everything was going along perfectly, Iverson said to himself, as his family celebrated Christmas 1992. He had just led Bethel High School's football team to the state championship, and the basketball team was undefeated. He was one of the most sought-after athletes in the United States. Coaches from Division I colleges flocked to his games to see him throw 60-yard touchdowns and sink 25-foot jump shots. He was going to have his pick of full-scholarship offers to a major college program; he was sure of it. This would guarantee him the chance to earn a good education, become a star, and win the fame and fortune that comes with such accomplishments.

Or so Allen thought. Never in his wildest nightmares could he have imagined the sequence of events about to befall him. They would threaten to destroy the world as he knew it, and possibly snatch from his grasp any chance to better his life and that of his family.

At 10 p.m. on Saturday, February 13, 1993, Allen and some friends went to the Circle Lanes bowling alley. It was near his home in Pine Chapel, one of the rougher housing projects in Hampton. After bowling a few frames, he and a buddy crossed the room to get something to eat. As they approached the snack bar, they were suddenly confronted by a group of white people from a nearby town. Words were exchanged; some say they included racial slurs. A punch was thrown. Someone yelled, "Fight, fight!" When things calmed down a few minutes later, a handful of the white people at the alley lay injured on the floor. Broken chairs, tables, and bottles littered the area.

Allen denied laying a hand on anyone, but several white witnesses identified him as being in the middle of the melee. The reason was simple: his athletic star status made him the most recognizable person in the room. The next day, he and several friends were picked up by police and charged with "maiming by mob." This was a little-used felony charge that, ironically, had been designed long ago as an anti-lynching law to combat the Ku Klux Klan.

Although Allen was only 17 years old and legally a juvenile, Virginia prosecutors chose to try him and his friend as adults. Many Iverson supporters claim this was political grandstanding by the prosecutor's office. But this charge was denied by state officials. The fact remains that in a melee of questionable beginnings, which involved more than 50 people, the only ones who were charged with any wrongdoing were four black teenagers. Of these, only Allen and his friend were charged with the most serious crimes.

Each boy was convicted and sentenced to 15 years in jail, but 10 years were suspended. Because of Iverson's sporting prowess and the racially charged nature of the case, it drew attention from coast to coast. Every major newspaper and national magazine covered the trial and its subsequent outcome. Tom Brokaw, of NBC News, chose to broadcast from Hampton and went so far as to conduct a jailhouse interview with Iverson.

Allen couldn't believe what was happening to him. It seemed like a horrible dream, he thought, as they led him away from the sentencing in handcuffs and leg shackles. He had done nothing wrong, but he was being treated like a criminal.

He had been convicted of a serious crime. His young life was shattered. In a flash, his senior year of high school was eliminated by a jail sentence. Now, he would never get his diploma. College? That was out of the question. And a scholarship? Who would ever believe his side of the story and take a chance on an ex-jailbird? He had lost everything, just because he had been in the wrong place at the wrong time. But to this day, Allen insists that he left the bowling alley as soon as the violence started.

Just when the situation looked darkest, as the college football scholarship offers were vanishing left and right, it was Iverson's mother who once again came through for her eldest child. Just as she had taught him a second game, when he was younger, to protect him from the physical punishment of football, now Ann Iverson made a last-ditch attempt to protect her son from the perils of a life in the ghetto. She picked up the phone and called John Thompson, head basketball coach at Georgetown University.

Ann had heard of his successful program that demanded discipline and emphasized academics. More important, she believed Thompson had the ability to get through to a boy from the streets and turn him into the man she could be proud of.

In the late 1970s, Thompson had taken over a program that was virtually unheard of. By applying an intense, hands-on coaching style, he stressed discipline and accountability that didn't stop when an athlete stepped off the court. The results were impressive, culminating in a national championship in 1984.

Georgetown regularly ranks among the top 25 in the nation, and its tradition of success attracts some of the country's most sought-after high-school players each recruiting season. Thompson is famous for getting the most he can out of the big guys—centers Patrick Ewing, Dikembe Mutombo, and Alonzo Mourning—but his knack for recognizing talent and shaping admirable young men knows no height restrictions.

Ann Iverson put the question to Thompson: Would he be willing to give her boy a chance when he got out of jail?

"Yes," Thompson said. "Let me come talk to him."

The very next day, Thompson and an assistant drove down to Hampton from Washington, D.C. They met with Allen and his mother for several hours. Thompson, a savvy recruiter, had been well aware of the boy's physical and athletic attributes. As a fresh, young basketball talent located practically in the coach's backyard, it would have been difficult for Thompson to ignore him. But the moral fiber of a Georgetown recruit is also important. Often, Thompson has declined to offer a scholarship to a player whose desire and commitment came into question. In Iverson's case, with his recent history, the intangible "character" issue was even more important to the coach.

Thompson questioned Allen at great length about the recent events in his life. He used every device he knew of to get the young man to reveal his inner self. The coach also conducted his own background checks through his well-developed network of sources. As he did so, Iverson's integrity and resolve became more and more evident.

It also helped that Allen respected the coach. "I wasn't a Georgetown fan when I was a kid, but

I was a Coach Thompson fan," he said later. He knew all about Thompson, all about the regimen and the military-style caring. The "whole person" program challenged Allen to bring out the best in himself.

Still, there were doubters. The negative publicity generated in the press about Iverson because of the bowling alley incident was formidable. Many people in the college and sporting communities thought he barely deserved common courtesy, much less a full scholarship to a prestigious university.

But Thompson is not one to be swayed by public opinion. When the deadline for offering scholarships arrived, he went with his gut. The young man was talented and committed. He deserved a chance. Thompson picked up the phone and dialed Allen's number.

Allen's legal luck also started to change. Instead of a state penitentiary, the judge in the case sentenced Allen to Newport News City Farm, a juvenile correction facility. Civil rights protests were creating an intense public scrutiny of the case. Virginia governor Douglas Wilder ordered his aides to look into the incident. And when they did, the governor decided to commute Iverson's sentence. After four months at the work farm, Allen and his friend were set free. Then, the convictions were overturned on appeal.

Once he was free, Allen knew that a high-school degree was his only chance of success. Exhibiting some of the resolve and responsibility he had learned from sports, he attended an alternative high school for at-risk youth and obtained his coveted diploma.

Finally, he was eligible for a college scholarship. Urged on by his mother, he jumped at Thompson's offer of a four-year deal.

4

A COACH'S
INFLUENCE

It wasn't easy at first. Early in his freshman year at Georgetown, Allen was just as likely to lead the team in turnovers as often as scoring. His lightning speed took not only opponents by surprise but his teammates as well. It took some time for everyone to get comfortable with his full-throttle style of play.

Fans at opposing venues were a problem. At away games, they were merciless. They taunted him about his jail time. Shouts of "jailbird" and "convict" filled the air.

But, slowly, with Thompson's patience, protection, and guidance, Allen blossomed. He took control of the Georgetown Hoyas and made them into *his* team.

Thompson was often criticized for allowing Iverson to take control of the team when he was a freshman before he got himself under control first. But Thompson saw something more than

Georgetown guard Allen Iverson drives between Morgan State's defenders in a November 30, 1994, game at Landover, Maryland.

Iverson moves to the basket, leaving Colgate's Malik Cupid (far left) and Jimmy Maloney (left) in the dust in the 1995 Pre-Season NIT Tournament at Landover, Maryland.

a brash, quicksilver-fast basketball player.

"A nontalented person is very easy to discipline," Thompson says. "People see somebody slow, who can't beat anybody on the drive, and I hear it all the time: 'Look at him, he's under control.' But, in fact, the guy can't move. He's not as fast as Allen, can't jump as high as Allen. When you've got the talent that Allen's got, it is much more difficult for you to restrict that. We disciplined Allen and lost some ball games. He needed to be free as a bird."

Iverson's affection and respect for his former coach is heartfelt.

"He taught me a lot of things: how to deal with people, how to deal with different situations, always to think 'life first' before anything. It made me feel good that he was comfortable with me. He always said he was comfortable with me on the basketball court, but he felt comfortable with me off the court as well. That meant a lot to me.

"It was good for me because Coach Thompson let me live. Everybody said different things about me before I got there [to Georgetown]—that I was going to be a troublemaker. But when I got there, Coach Thompson treated me like he treated everybody else. He might even have given me a little more freedom because that's the type of person I am. I'll do what I'm supposed to do, but just leave me alone and I'll get it done. Don't be scared of me or anything or think that I'm not going to do what I gotta do just because you give me freedom."

Like a sponge, Allen soaked up all of the lessons Thompson taught. They have left him in a good position to handle the tough times that often confront a person—on the basketball court and in life. His sparkling natural ability earned him honors as Freshman of the Year and Big East Defensive Player of the Year.

He improved even more as a sophomore. His scoring average increased from 20.4 points per game to a Big East best 25.0. His shooting accuracy increased from 39 percent to 48 percent. His decision-making ability on the court also got better. He harnessed his fast pace to accommodate his teammates and became a consensus first-team All-American. Once again, he won the Big East's top defender award.

With Iverson leading them, the Hoyas finished 21–10 in 1995, his first season, losing to the University of North Carolina in the National Collegiate Athletic Association (NCAA) Southeast Regional semifinal. Georgetown improved to 29–8 in 1996, losing to the University of Massachusetts in the East Regional title game. Before Iverson, Georgetown had not made consecutive regional semifinal appearances since 1984 and 1985, when it was led by Patrick Ewing.

Iverson also led the USA's gold medal basketball team in the 1995 World University Games. Playing with the likes of Wake Forest star Tim Duncan and the University of Connecticut's Ray Allen, Iverson was able to rein in his "shoot first" style en route to the title.

Iverson's development even garnered praise from opponents. "A lot of people have the phi-

West Virginia's Seldon Jeffer-
son (right) and Cyrus Jones
(left) watch as Iverson looks
to pass in first-half action
on December 2, 1995. The
Hoyas won in overtime,
86 to 83.

losophy of letting him get his and just shut the other guys off, but he's the kind of guy who can get beyond what you expect him to," says Memphis State coach Larry Finch, whose team has come out on the losing end of an Iverson-led team more often than he likes to admit. "He's more of a point shooter versus just being strictly a point guard, because he's looking to score, and Lord knows he can score. He hits baskets that are incredible."

Adds Nolan Richardson, coach of an NCAA champion team, the Arkansas Razorbacks: "I've seen three calf shows, nine horse ropings—I even saw Elvis once—but I've never seen a guard do what he can do with the basketball. I saw him go through traps of ours nobody's ever gone through. He's awesome."

With such heady praise in hand, Allen had no reason to be terribly upset when his last shot of the 1996 season clanked loudly off the rim in the waning seconds of the Hoyas' East Regional final loss to the University of Massachusetts. Exhausted, he walked off the court, but he could take solace in one thing: both he and the team had shown steady improvement.

"We'll be back next year," he vowed. "And next year we'll be the ones cutting down the net."

Once again, though, fate was waiting to step in and alter his carefully laid plans. Allen Iverson didn't know it at the time, but that 30-foot desperation attempt was to be his last shot ever in a Georgetown uniform.

5

THE DECISION TO TURN PRO

They were the most agonizing moments of his 18-year-old life.

When will that ambulance get here? Allen wondered. His mind raced frantically. The 911 dispatcher had said the emergency medical team would be there within five minutes, but it seemed like hours ago that he had hung up the phone. It was a race against time, and it was his baby sister's life that hung in the balance.

Just then, the door to the small apartment in Hampton, Virginia, burst open and the EMT squad snatched the unconscious baby from his arms. Allen fell back, feeling more helpless than he ever had before. If his football squad had been trailing by a touchdown with ten seconds on the clock, or his basketball team had been down by 20 points at the half, he would have known just what to do. But this wasn't a game, it was life. His baby sister, Aiesha, had suffered an attack

Iverson grabs the loose ball as Nick Bosnic tries to get back into play in a game against Duquesne on December 28, 1995. Georgetown won, 88 to 86.

of convulsions and there was nothing he could do about it. "Please, God, make her be all right," Iverson prayed.

The sound of a baby crying broke through his tortured thoughts. Aiesha was breathing again! A squad member said they were taking her to the hospital.

Allen's little sister survived that night in 1994, but she was diagnosed with a condition that caused periodic convulsions. It was like a terrible joke: the good news was that the convulsions could be controlled with medication; the bad news was that his mother couldn't always afford the medication. So, Allen made a pledge to himself: If he could ever do something to help his beloved baby sister, he would.

That was one of the reasons that, two years later, he was stepping up to a podium in the Georgetown athletic center. Looking out at the large gathering of reporters in front of him, he announced his decision to leave Georgetown after his sophomore year and make himself available for the NBA draft.

"My family needs me right now," he said. "I have an opportunity to take care of them."

Not only would the professional contract and the money it brought help his baby sister, it would also buy his mother and 16-year-old sister, Brandy, a nice house in a safe neighborhood.

"My immediate family requires that I leave Georgetown," Allen said, in closing. "But I'll always be part of the Georgetown family."

The decision drew a storm of criticism from the media. A college diploma is one of the most sought after, and expensive, documents in America. Not only can a diploma open doors in the business world, but the college experience itself can broaden your horizons and train you to think. More important, it can teach you about life. Here was Iverson, bystanders smirked, throwing away a free ride at a respected institution of higher learning—something others without his God-given ability to play basketball would give anything for.

Allen can understand the criticism, but to this day it doesn't make it any easier to accept. The decision to leave college early wasn't an easy one for him to make. He's used to finishing what he starts. After years of struggling with his grades, his academic career was flourishing in Georgetown's art department, where he was building upon an innate artistic talent.

Allen has always enjoyed an affinity for pencil and paper. He majored in art at Georgetown, and he lists drawing as a favorite pastime in the *Philadelphia 76ers' Media Guide*.

Childhood friend Dwayne Campbell remembers the first time he saw Allen pick up a pen and paper. "Just like that," he recounts, snapping his fingers, "Bubbachuck drew me a picture of Michael Jordan dunking over Dominique Wilkins. I had heard he could draw, but I had never seen him do it before. He just sat there and sketched it so fast— and it was perfect. I couldn't believe it."

Allen has an excellent head for business. He

Iverson picks up an offensive charge on a play against Syracuse defender J. B. Reafsnyder (left), in first-half action on February 10, 1996, at Syracuse.

realized that turning pro early didn't make sense; he would be a much more valuable and marketable commodity with four full seasons of college experience.

But, in his mind, he really had no choice at all. Momma and the babies needed his earning power now. If he waited two years, it might be too late. Meanwhile, his agent, David Falk, predicted that if he declared his eligibility, he would be one of the top five draft picks. In the market of the time, this decision could assure him a three-year contract worth approximately six million dollars. In addition, Reebok was dangling a forty-million-dollar endorsement deal, along with the pledge to manufacture a sneaker under his name. Who could resist that?

The All-American sophomore meets with reporters in Washington, D.C., on May 1, 1996, to announce he will quit Georgetown University and enter the NBA draft. Iverson became the first player under Coach John Thompson to leave early for the NBA.

Despite all this, deep down Allen agreed with the many observers who said he was, in reality, throwing away everything he had worked so hard for.

But it was *his* life, *his* reality. And there was no starker reality than waiting in the dead of night in a blackened apartment, an unconscious baby in your arms, begging God to let her live, and wishing the ambulance would get there faster.

6

REALIZING THE DREAM

Draft day, 1996.

As Allen slipped the Philadelphia 76ers' jersey over his head, the gravity of what had just happened hit him. He felt his heart catch in his throat. He had tried to prepare himself for this, but it overwhelmed him just the same. He was fulfilling a boyhood dream—the dream of nearly every child who had ever picked up a basketball in a playground.

Allen looked into the front row. Just off the stage stood his mother. She was the one who had taught him the simple game that would now enable him to earn a living. Tears were streaming down her face. But, at least, they were tears of happiness, Allen thought. There had been more than enough times in his brief life when the wetness on her face came from sorrow or disappointment, fear or frustration. It seemed like this small family had struggled most of its

The Philadelphia 76ers' Allen Iverson defends against the Boston Celtics' David Wesley during first-half action in Boston, January 22, 1997.

life to come to terms with one setback after another. The lack of running water or electricity. The lack of money to buy medicine for a sick baby. His wrongful arrest and conviction.

All of these thoughts came rushing into Allen's mind in the few seconds it took him to pull on that special jersey. And now it was over, in the past. Now, he was a Philadelphia 76er.

Then, the whirlwind began. Congratulations came from NBA commissioner David Stern, from 76ers president Pat Croce, and from his new coach, Johnny Davis. And, even more important, from Coach Thompson, who had made the trip to New York from Georgetown for the draft.

"You did the right thing," Thompson whispered into his ear as he hugged Allen. "And you'll do just fine. They'll be playing *your* game before too long."

This tortuous journey to the NBA might have destroyed a lesser man, but Iverson has retained an unshakable belief in himself and his ability. Confidence can't be lacking in a player who said he could beat Michael Jordan one-on-one—even if he said it while still in high school.

"I feel I can take Mike," Allen once told a high-school coach. Today, he still feels the same way. "He's just another basketball player. He's the best. But he's still just someone I have to face, and I feel confident about my game, no matter what."

It's not a lack of respect that motivates Allen but a total absence of fear. "You are a rookie and you come into the league and you are supposed to bow down? That's not me," he says. "Once you step on the hardwood, if you overrespect someone, the battle already has been lost."

"Allen is misunderstood at times," said Johnny Davis, the 76ers' coach during Iverson's rookie year, "mostly by people who don't know him. All

I can say is he's extremely coachable, he works hard, he plays hard, he does what I tell him. And his teammates love him."

At the time, Davis also brushed off any talk of selfish play, brought on by the fact that Iverson was leading the team in shots. "I think that comes from his confidence in his own abilities. He [takes the shot because he] thinks he can make the play. It's not because he's a selfish player."

Anyone who talks to Iverson for an extended period of time will see that winning as a team is the most important achievement he can imagine on the court. Early in his rookie year, he acknowledged his desire to win the Rookie of the

Iverson dives to save a loose ball from going out of bounds as the Miami Heat's P. J. Brown falls next to him during the first half of the February 18, 1997, game in Philadelphia.

Iverson looks to pass the ball as he splits the defense of the New Jersey Nets' Eric Montross (left) and Jim Jackson (right) during the first half of the game in East Rutherford, April 16, 1997. Iverson scored 27 points as the 76ers beat the Nets, 113 to 105.

Year Award, but he added that it wasn't his primary concern. "I would rather get to the playoffs than win the Rookie Award," he said. "That's an individual award and I would love to have [it], but it's not more important than achieving team goals, because I'm in a team game."

On a rebuilding team like the 76ers, Iverson sees his role as that of leader—in scoring and anything else that needs doing. "I do a lot of other things besides the scoring," Allen says. "I try to create for my teammates and create for myself. Scoring is just a big part of my game. . . . I don't think the Sixers would have selected me if they didn't want me to come in here and score."

"I think speed is everything," says Allen, who also sports a 40½-inch vertical leap. "As long as you are faster than somebody else, or just as fast, you can pretty much do what you want to do on the court.

"If you can go by guys in this league, you can make things happen, break a defense down. When I make a move, somebody has to come over and help out on defense, and when they do, they leave one of my teammates open for a pass. If they don't help out, I've got a bucket. I'm always, always looking to score. Always looking to try and make something happen."

Allen's flash and style on the court also make him a standout, and he does not deny bringing his old playground tricks and tactics into each game when necessary.

"You never know when you'll have to use something that you used in the street," he explains. "There are different situations. Defenders make you do things, and a lot of times I do things on instinct. It doesn't matter what game I am in. If it's a move I know how to do, then I do it—regardless of what it is. So I take everything I learned from the streets and put it in my NBA game."

One weapon in his bulging arsenal of tricks from the playground is a move that forced the NBA to alter how its referees call a game. Iverson's signature move is a crossover dribble that frees him to perform much of the magic that he makes. The move starts with him holding the ball in his right hand, daring the defender to go for it. When the defender commits himself, Iverson dribbles behind his back, leaving the opponent grasping at nothing but air. He accomplishes the move with such blinding speed that the NBA decided he must be carrying the ball. The league office went so far as to issue a directive to all officials, as well as the 76ers, stating that a traveling penalty would be called each time he used it unless it was modified.

"They aren't accustomed to seeing it, so they call it a violation," said Davis. "He does it so quickly. He's so versatile that the refs can't believe he's doing it legally. They are saying his hand is underneath the ball. It's not."

Since then, Allen has modified the move, but it is no less effective.

"Once you go for the ball, it's over," says Cleveland Cavalier forward Donnie Marshall. As a player at the University of Connecticut, he regularly played against Allen in college. "He'll step back on you or go to the hole and dunk on you. He's the most explosive six-foot point guard you've ever seen."

Not since Shaquille O'Neal entered the league in 1992 has a rookie scored so much. And not since Michael Jordan turned pro in 1984 has a guard averaged more than 23 points a game in his first season.

"He runs the ball down your throat and makes things happen," Portland's Kenny Anderson says of Iverson. "He just takes it to everybody. He's got that confidence, that cockiness, that nastiness, that you have to have to make it in this league."

These attributes are just some of the reasons many say Iverson is the best among a new breed of NBA point guard—quick, small, and offensive-minded. In the recent past, teams have stressed a sizable backcourt, with players such as the 6'9" Earvin "Magic" Johnson, Dennis Johnson, and Anfernee "Penny" Hardaway as the prototype. If he can continue his recent success, Iverson, and a cadre of other players barely six feet tall, such as Atlanta's Mookie Blaylock, Cleveland's Terrell Brandon, and Minnesota's Stephon Marbury, could send NBA scouts rushing to sign players of smaller stature.

"I always wanted to be a scorer," Allen says. "That's just something I was born with. God gave me the ability to put the ball in the hoop. My size didn't allow me to become a two guard in the league, so I had to play point guard. But I feel I do a lot of things besides scoring."

Marty Blake, the NBA's director of scouting, calls Iverson the fastest he's seen in his 45-year affiliation with the league.

"He's as quick with the ball as anyone in the history of the game," the 76ers' Davis said. "He's a combination of Isiah Thomas and Tiny Archibald [NBA all-stars of the eighties]. He makes fast guys in this league look slow. He has a level beyond their quickness."

"Allen reminds me of Isiah, because he can take over a game," added the Sixers' assistant coach, Maurice Cheeks, himself a former championship-winning point guard. "Allen's ability to beat people off the dribble is going to bring defenders to him. He's starting now to make the extra pass, and his assist total is starting to rise."

Nowhere was Iverson's leadership more in evidence than during the 1997 Rookie All-Star Game, in Cleveland. As usual in out-of-town arenas, a smattering of boos could be heard through the applause during the pregame player introductions.

"I'll show them," Allen thought to himself. And he did.

In a game that pitted him against the players that will be his peers for the next decade or more, he played with a vengeance. A three-pointer here, a lightning fast, no-look pass there, a snared rebound among much taller forwards and centers. He dominated the action, scoring 19 points, dishing out nine assists, blocking three shots, and making three steals, en route to leading the East rookies to a 96–91 win over the West squad. For his efforts, he was awarded the game's Most Valuable Player Award.

He left the court to a standing ovation.

7

THE BIG LEAGUES

"**S**pecial. He's going to be very, very special."

Early in Iverson's NBA career, his former coach at Georgetown, John Thompson, uttered those prophetic words.

"Allen is going to be a great player, not a typical point guard," Thompson noted before Iverson's professional debut. "Typical point guards don't make it into the NBA. In Allen, what Philadelphia got is a player with great intelligence, speed, and unusual endurance. What he doesn't have is experience. That only comes from playing. He'll get that in time. While he was at Georgetown, he soaked up everything. He'll continue to do the same here [in the pros]. And when he gets that experience, he'll be incredible."

The proof came quicker than anyone, except possibly Allen himself, could have expected—in his first professional regular season game, in

The East Team's Allen Iverson, of the Philadelphia 76ers, holds the MVP trophy after the NBA Rookie game, February 8, 1997, in Cleveland. Iverson scored 19 points to lead the East to a 96–91 win.

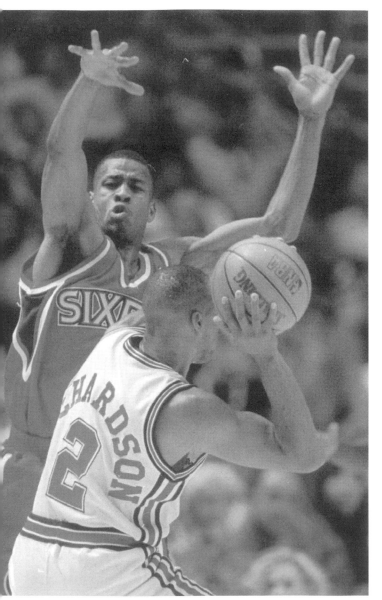

Iverson guards Pooh Rich-ardson, of the Los Angeles Clippers, during the first half of their exhibition game, October 22, 1996, in Anaheim, California.

Milwaukee. The feeling was electrifying for the 21-year-old. Instead of intimidating the rookie—which was the hoped-for effect—the roar of the hostile crowd, the high-decibel, throbbing music, and the bright laser lights that characterize big-time professional sports events energized him. Like a racehorse straining at the bit, Allen felt ready to prove, once and for all, that he belonged with the best players in the world.

The game started slowly. Both teams circled each other warily like a pair of boxers, tentatively probing for a weakness. Then, with about two minutes gone off the clock, Allen took an inbounds pass and made his way up court. Now is the time, he told himself—time to show everyone what I've got and see if they can stop me.

He circled to his right, dribbling slowly, drawing the man guarding him far to the side of the court. Then, after a quick head and shoulder fake to the left, he cut down low along the baseline and easily drove around his man toward the basket. For a moment, he saw nothing but a clear path to the hole. He planted his left leg and sprang for the basket. Just after he let the ball go, he was jarred by a heavy object coming from his left and was slammed to the hardwood.

Kneeling under the basket, he tried to catch the breath that had just been knocked out of his body. When he looked up, he saw Glenn "Big Dog" Robinson, a former first-round draft pick and one of the Bucks' forwards, grinning down at him.

Welcome to the big leagues, kid.

Allen picked himself up off the floor, put the confrontation behind him, and went on that night to score a game-high 30 points. He had met the test and prevailed. Unfortunately, his elation was tempered by the fact that his performance came in an eight-point loss.

Two nights later, on November 8, 1996, he led the 76ers to his first victory as a professional, a 115–105 win over the Boston Celtics. Allen scored 32 points, 15 in the fourth quarter, drawing praise from at least one opponent.

"He goes in there so fearlessly," said an admiring Dana Barros, the Celtic guard assigned to cover Iverson. Nevertheless, Barros questioned whether the slight Iverson, at six feet and 165 pounds, will be able to withstand the steady physical pounding of an 82-game NBA regular season. "Teams with a strong defensive presence are going to hit him and won't let him come down the lane."

But Allen is unconcerned. "If you can't take the punishment, you need to sit on the bench," he says. "And sitting on the bench isn't for me."

He backed up this tough talk with some tough play. He averaged 30.5 points in two November wins over the New York Knicks, a rugged team noted for its tight defense and physical play. In the course of the first Knicks game, Iverson succeeded in fouling out Charlie Ward and Scott Brooks, who were sent to guard him. Then, two weeks later, he fouled out Chris Childs and drew five fouls on backup John Starks.

"I didn't make it easy for him, but when a guy has that much freedom and control to do what he wants, he's difficult to guard," observed Ward after the first contest. "I tried to stay in front of him and keep him out of the paint the best I could." But it was not good enough.

Allen's performance in the second Knicks game was even more impressive—because he wasn't scheduled to play. A separated shoulder suffered less than five days earlier had forced the rookie to miss two games, but he declared himself able to play against the Knicks.

"It hurt more emotionally to just sit and watch the previous night's game," Allen said later. "I felt my teammates needed me, and I couldn't help them. I sat up all night [before the Knicks game] icing the shoulder. When I told my friends I was going to play, they looked at me like I was crazy, [but] when the doctor gave me the OK, I was ready to roll."

Allen lit up the visiting New Yorkers with 26 points, and just missed a triple double, handing out nine assists and pulling down nine rebounds to go with his game-high point total.

"There's no quit in him," teammate Derrick Coleman commented. "His tempo is go, go, go."

Allen Iverson always has been the type of player to rise to a challenge. He is able to take his game to yet another, higher level when the competition demands it. As proof, he hung a 24-point performance on another quick guard to whom he is often compared, the Toronto Raptors' Damon Stoudamire. In addition, he scored 81 points in two games his first year against the world champion Chicago Bulls.

But, still, the criticism that he shoots too much continues to haunt him.

"You see other point guards put up big numbers, so I don't know why they criticize me so much about shooting," Allen says. "But I guess that comes with being Allen Iverson. I wish I wasn't the one singled out. It's just another obstacle in my life, something I have to deal with."

Pat Croce, the 76ers' president, is ready to let him do what is necessary to overcome the criticism. Although he predicts a long learning curve for his budding star, Croce seems ready to wait. "He has been on his own his whole life. He's used to trial and error."

Croce is resolved to be patient with his 21-year-old multimillionaire star as he learns from his mistakes. "The turnovers make you cringe, but that's part of the package," Croce acknowledges.

The "package," as he calls Iverson's game, features an explosive first step to the basket that could be the quickest in the game. It has produced statistics that place Iverson in the upper echelon of the league: a sixth-place ranking in points per game, with a 25.5 scoring average, and seventh in steals per game (2.07). And despite the charges of selfishness, Iverson ranked eleventh in the NBA in assists per game (7.5), including a career high of 15 against the Boston Celtics on April 18, 1997.

Necessity has led to much of Iverson's flashy offensive output. Unfortunately, the 76ers are in

Washington Bullets' Rod Strickland (left) loses control of the ball as he gets by Iverson in the first half of the April 14, 1997, game in Philadelphia.

Pat Croce (center), the Philadelphia 76ers' owner, jokes with players Iverson and Jerry Stackhouse (right) during media-day activities at Bob Carpenter Center, in Newark, Delaware, October 3, 1996.

the middle of a long rebuilding process. The team, at one point during Iverson's rookie 1996–97 season, lost 18 of 19 games, and they finished with a 22–60 record—the fifth worst in the league and only four games better than the previous year's 18–64 record.

Nevertheless, with Iverson and fellow guard Jerry Stackhouse, himself a first-round pick in 1995, there is room for optimism. The team heads into the 1997–98 campaign with a new coach, Larry Brown. A proven veteran coach, recently of the Indiana Pacers, Brown has a history of success with young teams.

Brimming with optimism, Allen heartily endorses the moves the team has made to strengthen itself. But he clearly sees his leadership role.

"Point guards can do so many things," he says. "They can get others involved; they can get themselves involved. You add a lot to a team if you are a point guard, and you can score, too. Of course, you can pass the ball, hit people, get people open, but if the opposition is worrying about your scoring ability as well, that makes you that much stronger."

It's important to understand that Iverson is still learning. And the most important thing he has learned from his first year in the league is patience.

"Similar to college, it took me a little while to get adjusted. I was trying to do so many things, trying to show everybody that I can play instead of letting it come to me and being patient. I have to remember to get everybody involved, make sure I get them their shots," he acknowledges.

Record-setting performances are not a bad first step toward earning the respect of your peers and the patience of the owner. What really impresses is the nature of the record Allen set by breaking the 40-point barrier in five consecutive games. It wasn't just a one-time event, like a single-game scoring or a rebounding high—it was top performance over an extended stretch. His tenacity is further reflected in playing time that averaged 40.1 minutes a game. Despite the pounding he takes from much larger opponents, he missed only six games his first season.

"I went through a lot of things to test my manhood. I'm glad—not glad, really, but stronger for it—that all of those things happened to me. I feel like I can handle anything. I learned a lot about people, about how things can change. No matter who you are, when somebody wants to bring you down, he can do it. Everything you worked for can be all over in a moment."

REPAYING
A DEBT

Despite his new-found wealth and celebrity, Allen Iverson stays close to his roots. He travels and lives with a small group of friends he has known since childhood. Although some see the "Iverson Posse," as the group is sometimes called, as a possible bad influence because of their questionable backgrounds, Iverson views the support of his friends as loyalty.

"When I was struggling growing up, no running water in my house, the electric lights turned off, these were the guys who were with me," Allen explains. "They grew up with me. I'm not going to turn my back on them now. Not many people were always angels as they grew up. These are the guys who won't always be telling me how great I am. They know me.

"I don't worry about impressing anyone," he

76er Allen Iverson is congratulated by his proud mother, Ann, after winning the NBA Rookie of the Year Award, May 1, 1997, in Philadelphia. He received 44 of 115 votes from the sportswriters and broadcasters who cover the NBA.

adds. "I don't care what people say. The people who count to me are my family and friends. The rest of the people, they're going to think what they think."

Because of the many difficult situations he has found himself in over the years, Allen's heart goes out to those in trouble or in need.

Recently, Allen repaid a lifelong debt to the man he calls "Dad," the man who helped his mother raise him. He is someone Allen refers to in the loving tones he usually reserves for his closest confidants and family. This is a man who has battled addiction for most of his life and almost succumbed one recent winter night.

In February 1997, the 76ers were in the middle of a West Coast road trip when Allen was roused from a deep sleep. Groggy from the effects of jet lag and the strain of playing three games in four days, he fumbled in the dark of the hotel room to silence the harsh jangle of the telephone. Picking up the receiver, he mumbled, "Hello."

Suddenly, he was jerked wide awake. It was his mother on the other end of the line. She was crying. Dad had started taking drugs again and was creating a disturbance. What if one of the neighbors called the police and they came and arrested him? What should she do?

Allen tried to calm down his mother. He fixed the immediate problem by giving her the name of a friend to call. The friend would come and quiet down Dad and smooth things over with the neighbors. The Sixers were returning east in a few days, and he would come home to see to the problem himself.

Staring into the blackness of the hotel room, Allen came to a grim realization: because Dad had been convicted several times for selling drugs, another arrest probably would mean hard jail time for him. Despite his one weakness, he was a genuinely good person. He had stood by Allen during some of the darkest periods of his life.

Once again, just when he least expected it, just when his life finally seemed to be turning into the fairy tale that the media and his friends already thought it was, fate had stepped in and slapped him in the face with reality. Once again, he was being asked to take on responsibility more suited to an older, wiser person than a 21-year-old.

But if there is one thing Allen Iverson has learned in his short life, it is to expect the un-expected—and accept it. He recalled something that this man who now needed his help so des-perately had once said to him.

It was when Allen was a teenager, complain-ing that his mother was making him do some-thing he didn't want to do.

"I'm a man now," Allen raged. "I can score over the baddest dude on the court and everyone on the playground respects me. She can't disrespect me by treating me like a child."

"Allen," Dad said, "being a man isn't being able to do anything you want to do, it's doing what you have to do."

As Allen lay back now in the hotel bed, in a vain attempt to grab a few precious hours of sleep before the team bus came to take him to the airport, he knew what he had to do. Just as he stepped up on the court every night to shoul-der the burden of leading his team to victory, he had to step up and accept this newest challenge and responsibility.

A week later, in early March 1997, Dad entered one of the country's best substance-abuse re-habilitation clinics, courtesy of basketball star Allen Iverson.

Giving of his time and money is important to Allen Iverson, giving not only to friends and family but to those less fortunate than himself. Because he believes in this so strongly, he is a willing participant in NBA and Philadelphia 76ers charities.

The NBA supports Black History Month, CARE, the National Committee To Prevent Child Abuse, and the Reading Is Fundamental program. In addition, the Sixers have teamed up with several Philadelphia-area youth organizations to recognize structured programs in education, recreation, and community service.

Because he grew up in a single-parent home, without his true biological father, Allen is a particularly soft touch for children's issues and programs such as the Big Brothers/Big Sisters organization. More than most, he understands the need for a strong male role model for children, particularly in the African-American community. He makes countless public appearances at charity events and often hosts underprivileged youth for games at the CoreStates Center, the 76ers' home arena. He also contributes memorabilia for charity auctions and participates in the Sixers Slam Dunk Diabetes Holiday Festival every Thanksgiving. This event raises money to fight juvenile diabetes.

As for life after basketball, Allen thinks he might develop his other talent and love: art.

Boo Williams is an old adviser and teacher who runs the summer basketball league in Hampton, Virginia. He feels that Allen could have found a career as a draftsman or an artist if basketball had not worked out.

"I believe that an artist, whether a singer, dancer, painter, or athlete, is multitalented," Williams says. "There is something special within them. A God-given ability that can come out in so many ways."

Williams predicts that Allen's talent will manifest itself eventually in other forms.

Pencils and paint are fine, but right now Allen Iverson's main tool of self-expression is his body and a basketball, and his easel is the entire NBA.

"This is my profession. I want to be the best," Allen proclaims. "Years from now, when people are talking about Magic and Michael, I want my name to be mentioned, too. I have a lot of work to do, but that's what I want."

Iverson sets to throw a football in the Philadelphia Eagles' practice bubble, January 30, 1997. He was "trying out" for the team as a quarterback, his position in high school, as part of the team's weekly TV show.

STATISTICS

COLLEGE STATISTICS
Georgetown University

YEAR	G	PTS	PPG	REB	RPG	B	BPG	AST	APG	STL
1994–95	30	613	20.4	99	3.3	5	.17	134	4.5	89
1995–96	37	926	25.0	141	3.8	16	.43	173	4.7	124
Totals	67	1,539	23.0	240	3.6	21	.31	307	4.6	213

PROFESSIONAL STATISTICS
Philadelphia 76ers

YEAR	G	PTS	PPG	REB	RPG	B	BPG	AST	APG	STL
1996–97	76	1,787	23.5	312	4.1	24	.32	567	7.5	157
1997–98	80	1,758	22.0	296	3.7	25	.31	494	6.18	176
1998–99	48	1,258	26.8	236	4.9	7	.15	223	4.65	110
1999–00	70	1,989	28.4	267	3.8	5	.07	328	4.69	144
2000–01	50	1,515	30.3	204	4.1	16	.32	240	4.80	120
Totals	274	6,818	24.9	1,111	4.1	61	.22	1,612	5.88	587

G   games
PTS   points
PPG   points per game
REB   rebounds
RPG   rebounds per game
B   blocks
BPG   blocks per game
AST   assists
APG   assists per game
STL   steals

Allen Iverson
A Chronology

1975	Born June 7, Hampton, Virginia
1983	Introduced to basketball by mother, Ann
1990	First dunk in organized basketball game
1993	Arrested and convicted following melee in bowling alley. After serving four months at Newport News City Farm, sentence is commuted by Governor Wilder and conviction is overturned on appeal
1994	Accepts scholarship from Georgetown University, Washington, D.C.
1995	Led U.S. team to gold medal in World University Games
1995–96	Selected Big East Defensive Player of the Year in each of his two seasons at Georgetown; led Hoyas in scoring in each of his two seasons (20.4 points per game as freshman, 25 points per game as sophomore); set single-season Georgetown record with 124 steals as a sophomore; holds Hoyas' freshman record with 89 steals
1996	Named first team All-American by Associated Press as a college sophomore. First player chosen overall in NBA draft, by Philadelphia 76ers
1996–97	NBA All-Rookie First Team; Rookie of the Month for November 1996 and April 1997; led all rookies in scoring with 1,787 points—293 more than runner-up Shareef Abdur-Rahim of Vancouver (even though he played four fewer games)
1997	Wins Schick Rookie of the Year Award; during the off-season, arrested when Virginia police found a handgun and marijuana in a car he was riding in; sentenced to three years probation and 100 hours of community service
1999	Iverson leads the NBA in scoring for the 1998-99 season
2001	Iverson named MVP in the NBA All-Star Game, during which Iverson scores 25 points to give the East a 111-110 win over the West (15 of the 25 points were scored in the final nine minutes of the game)

FURTHER READING

Broussard, Chris. "It Seems Nothing Can Stop Sixers' Iverson." *Delaware State News*, November 15, 1996.

Brown, Clifton. "Iverson Is the Philadelphia Story As 76ers Beat Knicks." *The New York Times*, November 13, 1996.

Cawthon, Raad. "Iverson Boosts Sixers Past Knicks." *The Philadelphia Inquirer*, November 24, 1996.

DeCourcy, Mike. "With Iverson, the Hoyas Are Every Team's Horror." *The Sporting News*, March 11, 1996.

Dwyer, Timothy. "On Allen Iverson." Knight-Ridder/Tribune News Service, June 27, 1996.

Falkner, David. "The Agony and the Ecstasy." *The Sporting News*, January 30, 1995.

Ford, Bob. "Iverson Is Chosen As MVP of the Rookie All-Star Game." *The Philadelphia Inquirer*, February 9, 1997.

Isola, Frank. "Allen King." *New York Daily News*, November 13, 1996.

"Iverson's 32 Lift Sixers to Victory." *Reading Times*, November 9, 1996.

Jasner, Phil. "Fast Start Earns Iverson Rookie of Month Honors." *Philadelphia Daily News*, December 4, 1996.

———. "Sixers Make Iverson No. 1 Draft Pick." Knight-Ridder/Tribune News Service, June 27, 1996.

Johnson, Paul M. "The Answer." *Sport*, March 1997.

MacMullan, Jackie. "Growing Teams." *Sports Illustrated*, January 20, 1997.

———. "A Matter of Respect." *Sports Illustrated*, February 17, 1997.

Mitchell, John N. "Thompson: Iverson Will Be 'Special.'" *Delaware State News*, November 2, 1996.

Montville, Leigh. "Flash Point." *Sports Illustrated*, December 9, 1996.

Powell, Shaun. "To All Iverson Bashers: Give Him a Break." *The Sporting News*, February 24, 1997.

Teel, David. "Citing Family's Needs, Iverson Says He Will Enter NBA Draft." Knight-Ridder/Tribune News Service, May 1, 1996.

Whyte, Kenneth. "Missing a Good Game." *Saturday Night,* May 1995.

Wojciechowski, Gene. "Iverson Has a Clearer Lane after Appeals Court Ruling." *The Sporting News,* July 3, 1995.

ABOUT THE AUTHOR

CHARLES E. SCHMIDT JR., a lifelong sports fan and native of eastern Pennsylvania, covered high school and college sports for nine years at the *Express-Times* newspaper, in Easton, Pennsylvania. He currently lives in the Chicago area, where he is a public affairs specialist for a national trade association.

PICTURE CREDITS:

AP/Wide World Photos: 2, 8, 16, 18, 26, 28, 30, 32, 35, 36, 38, 41, 42, 46, 48, 51, 52, 54, 59; Hampton Daily Press: 12.

INDEX

796.323092   Schmidt Charles E.
SCH   ALLEN IVERSON